Morning sunlight bathes terraced crops of winter wheat and barley in a soft, wondrous light. These are the terraced slopes of the Chilime Khola that rises high on the flanks of Ganesh Himal and throws its waters southeast to join the Trisuli River.

It is *Tihar*, the Festival of Light and harvest thanksgiving. Decorated lengths of bamboo sway and arch in the autumn winds and garlands of flowers and leaves reach over homes, bridges and water points to appease the spirits of the land and so ensure fertility, good monsoons and a safer tomorrow. (Takum-Sibang, Myangdi Khola, W. Nepal.)

Opposite: A small Thakali boy still wears the earrings of his youth and smiles winsomely as he leaves for school near Lete on the Kali Gandaki River, W. Nepal. Powerful and dramatic rejuvenation of this great river will soon destroy his home and village.

Publisher: Col. B.M. Niven
Thomson 808, #19-22
Thomson 800, Thomson Rd
Singapore 298190
Tel: (65) 2544189

Printed by C.O.S. Printers Pte Ltd,
Singapore
ISBN No.: 981-04-3909-1
Copyright©2001 B.M. Niven
First Edition. April 2001

PHOTOGRAPHY:
All photographs in this book were taken by the author using Leica cameras loaded with Kodachrome 64 film. The Panoramas were taken using a Hasselblad Xpan camera and Kodachrome 64 film. No filters or artificial light sources were used.

THE
MOUNTAIN
KINGDOM

VOLUME 2

The Gurkhas
and their
Homeland

The Photographs of
Colonel Bruce Niven

Go as a pilgrim midst the cathedrals of the great mountains
And climb the snows of that last glistening pass.
There, in the mystical pre-dawn light, acknowledge the Sun-god
And feel the awful presence of the forces of life.
Look out across far-flung banner clouds
To summits steeped in sun-flushed glory… and then look downwards
And wonder at the rugged beauty of a Kingdom spread below.

Descend to beaten earth of simple homesteads set on steep and rocky land
And meet there with warrior hillmen and rugged mountain folk.
As a privilege, enjoy the hospitality, generosity and gentleness so freely given,
And envy at the hardy dignity, proud resilience and enduring bravery
Of the people of this land.

Be grateful that you came this way and met these people,
For they gave you much, buoyed you up and were your life.

Colonel B.M. Niven

Dawn in the pass of Jalja-La. The pass leads down west into the Dhorpatan Plain and the headwaters of the Uttar Ganga River. The sun strikes through the mountain rhododendron trees and the prayer flags that mark the shrine in the pass. The valley below is filled with dense grey cloud, flushed pink by the Sun-god and above the clouds is laid out the still dark form of the Annapurna complex with a banner cloud proudly streaming from the summit of the highest peak, Annapurna I.

The early morning winter sun shafts into the cold, deep valley of the Sinja Khola. The bridge spans the river and lies on the main trail between Jumla and Rara Lake in high N.W. Nepal.

Prelude

The preparation of this book has been a labour of love born out of my forty years of service with Gurkhas and my knowledge of their Homeland. As a commander I knew from early on in my service that to understand my men in depth I needed to master their culture and crisscross their Homeland on foot.

My first book on Nepal – The Mountain Kingdom: Portraits of Nepal and the Gurkhas – was first published in 1987. The book is well illustrated and consists of seven chapters. It seeks to explain why the Gurkha is what he is and how young Gurkhas who come forward to be recruited are already imbued with sterling qualities unavailable to those not born as yeoman hill farmers in the shadow of giant mountains far from comfort and the well-lit avenues of life. The first five chapters of the book set the scene while the final two take the reader into the regiments, enabling him to understand how young Gurkha recruits are moulded into the world's finest infantry. Good leadership and dedicated trainers are of course vital ingredients in the process.

This, my second book, is a photographic essay and is meant as a companion volume to the first one. I have determined not to repeat anything and this time to let my photographs speak for themselves. I have, however, written captions for those thirsting for explanation and direction. The book is set out in three main parts: The Homeland, The Gurkhas and Final Impressions. It is for the viewer to gaze into the photographs the better to understand my love for Nepal and its people.

The human qualities Gurkhas bring to soldiering are unique and are determined by their upbringings as hill boys in a demanding and often harsh environment. Once he has accepted you, the kindness, generosity and companionship that emanate from the Gurkha are deep and meaningful. As soldiers they are utterly professional in everything that they do. Their discipline is awesome and their single-minded devotion to duty and the job in hand is respected by all who serve with them and not least by those who would oppose them. Their fighting spirit and resilience in battle are legendary as are their compassion, gentleness and ready laughter once the battle's o'er.

And so this book is a tribute to unique groups of mountain men who come forward as warriors and serve with an earnestness, panache and elan that stimulate their allies, cow their adversaries and confound their critics.

I will never adequately be able to repay my personal debt to those with whom I served.

Khabardar ra baliyo rahanu hos…
Remain vigilant and strong…

Colonel B.M. Niven
Singapore 2001

THE HOMELAND
Annapurna

It is sunrise in the Modi Khola, south of Annapurna and a few hours short of the Annapurna Base Camp on this, the southern side. The sun's rays strike obliquely off the great black pyramid of rock that is Machhapuchhare and then sheer skywards. To the left (rear), the mountain still in shadow is Gangapurna and the white tip of Annapurna III is just visible over the right shoulder of Machhapuchhare.

(Left) And sunrise a day later - Machhapuchhare as seen from the Annapurna Base Camp.

Above: The great mass of Dhaulagiri I dominates the skyline and causes an expedition member en route Annapurna I to pause, gather breath and admire the sheer majesty of the scene. *Right & Bottom Right*: Two stalwart porters, each carrying a heavy load of mountaineering kit and equipment on a *namlo*, or head strap, arrive safely at the Annapurna Base Camp after the long, arduous crossing of the Thulo Bugin Pass.

Opposite: Captain Henry Day R.E. above the clouds at Camp 2 during the successful climb of Annapurna I by the British Army team. Captain Day was the lead climber and is seen here on a mountain radio just prior to the successful summit bid. The snow-clad mass of 'La Grande Barrière' rises in the background.

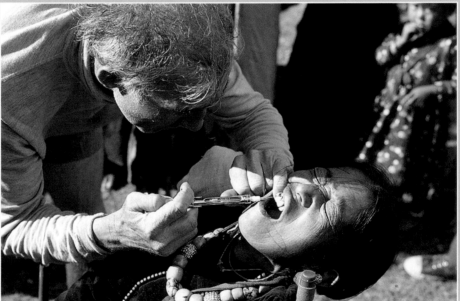

Top: David Jones, the doctor with the British and Nepalese Army expedition, anticipating lunch, cautiously lets off steam from a pressure cooker at Camp 2 during the climb. *Above*: He turns dentist and does a bit of 'hearts and minds' work amongst the villagers during the expedition's approach march to Annapurna. *Opposite*: The young Pertemba Sherpa, out with the British and Nepalese Army team on his very first major expedition as a high-altitude climber, smiling here from the sanctuary of his tent. Pertemba was to go on and become an illustrious climbing *Sirdar* (lead Sherpa) in his own right and still leads expeditions to the Himalayas.

Annapurna

A very large, powdered avalanche engulfs the basin and upper reaches of the Annapurna Glacier. The avalanche has broken off and come down from the huge 'sickle' hanging glacier that dominates the entire northwestern approach to the summit. This view of the summit was as seen by the French expedition under Maurice Herzog when it successfully scaled the Mountain in 1950 – the very first peak of 8,000m ever to have been climbed anywhere in the world. The British and Nepalese Army expedition made only the second successful climb of Annapurna I when it followed in Herzog's footsteps and reached the summit in May 1970. *Inset*: The mountain in a quieter mood – a wisp of snow spume and blown ice crystals rises from the summit.

The Rolwaling

Right: A Tamang shepherd boy enjoys the early morning sun on the steps of his home. His homespun woollen jacket helps to fend off the cold winds of winter as he tends his flock of goats on the grazing grounds above his home in Bulung Gaun on the Tamba Kosi River, E. Nepal. *Below*: A sturdy Tamang lad weaves his way homeward with a heavy load of thorny leaves as food for his cows and goats. A bundle of straw protects his neck and shoulders from thorns.

Opposite: A Rolwaling porter ties up his load with skill and dexterity and enjoys a locally rolled cigarette before hoisting the load for the long haul up to the lamasery at Beding.

Top: The author's Sherpa companions return from a reconnaissance of Ramdung Peak and (*above*) from the author's tent high up on Ramdung Himal, the late evening jet winds are seen tearing at the summit of Kang Nachugo.

The lamasery at Beding. Situated on a river terrace just above the erratic and turbulent flow of the Rolwaling River, the lamasery is forever threatened by powerful surges of water that scour downstream when glacier lakes situated above Beding collapse to release millions of litres of trapped water. Such surges do enormous damage and scour the landscape of buildings, bridges, shrines and prayer walls.

Above: Manaslu. The splendour of this mighty 8,000m peak is clearly seen from the trailside close to the upper reaches of the Buri Gandaki River near Sama Gompa. The northern glacier and icefall plunge down towards the trail and the early morning thermal winds move a slight cloud of blown snow from off the twin North and South Summits of this giant mountain.

The Buri Gandaki and Manaslu

The golden colours of mid-autumn flush through the green coniferous trees on the mountain slopes above Sama Gaun. The simple homesteads are capped with fire smoke and the stacked barley sheaves cast long shadows in the early morning light.

In the shadow of Manaslu a weak dawn sun begins to
light up a tributary valley of the Buri Gandaki River.

With the near padi terraces still stepped out in total darkness, the sun reaches into this eastern valley of the Buri Gandaki near the villages of Keronja and Kasi Gaun to highlight fields of green wheat and the brilliant yellow of the mustard fields. These two villages lie on the high, northern route between Gorkha and Trisuli Bazaar, W. Nepal.

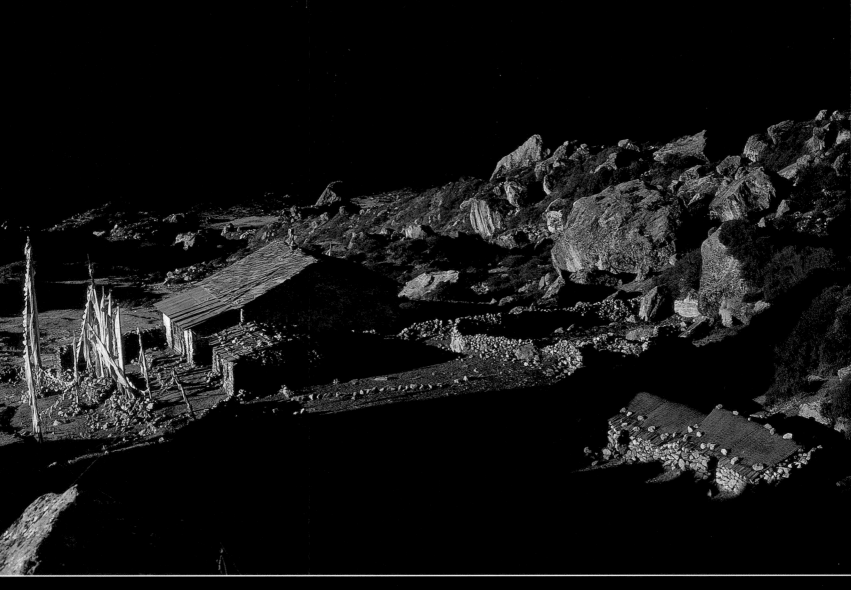

The oblique, early rays of the dawn sun strike the buildings, prayer walls and prayer flags of the lamasery at Kyangjin. Buddhist devotees built their lamasery here amidst the boulders and glacier debris of the Lantang Lirung Glacier.

Opposite(Top):Near the Ganja-La Pass, light begins to penetrate the Lantang Valley and picks out the sands of the glacier outwash plain that flanks parts of the

Top: A thick layer of hoarfrost covers the ground in a sparkling display at this settlement just beyond the sacred lake of Gosainkund. The skyline is dominated by the many majestic summits of Ganesh Himal that are ranged around the high central node of Ganesh I and Pabil. *Above*: This valley flanks Ganesh Himal and is still in deep shadow but the autumn colours of the trees and the mountain grasses emerge triumphantly in the morning sun above the Chilime Khola as the last vestiges of early morning mist disperse into an azure sky.

Opposite: Two heavily laden porters ascend a rock staircase to traverse a steep spur on the Chilime Khola that drains the eastern basin of Ganesh Himal. The staircase is built by herdsmen out of boulders and rocks taken from the river to enable them each spring to take their flocks up onto the high pastures.

The backview onto the Dhaulagiri complex as seen
from the pilgrimage centre at Muktinath at the head
of the Kali Gandaki River, W. Nepal. The huge walls
of the highest peak – Dhaulagiri I at 8,000m and
capped here by a banner cloud – can clearly be seen.
The other main peak making up the central node is
Tukuche Himal. Muktinath's shrines and eternal
flame are sacred to both Hindus and Buddhists. The
festoons of prayer flags that deck out the area hang
limp and dark in the still, deep shadow.

Opposite: A Puneni on the verandah of her
homestead. Ulleri, W. Nepal.

A view past the Tukuche Lamasery and its religious trappings and small outhouses up towards the vast slab of bare, scoured rock that is the great eastern wall of Tukuche Himal.

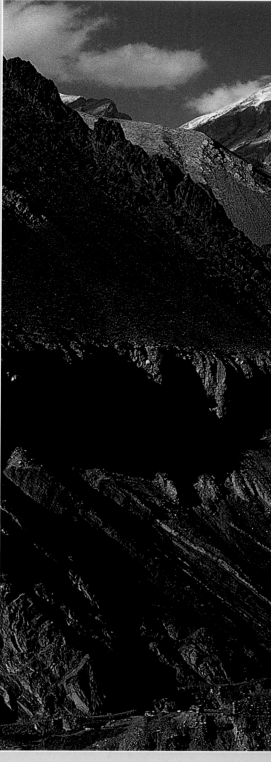

The settlement of Kagbeni at the head of the Kali Gandaki River close to Mustang. The red and white walls of the *gompa* (lamasery) stand out clearly. The landscape lies in the rain shadow of the Himalayas and only the hardiest of plants can survive the intense cold and lack of rain. Patch-fields seek out the warmth and moisture of the valley bottom to produce meagre crops of hardy cereals and potatoes. Kagbeni is a main gateway to Tibet and lies on what was at one time the major route for the vital trade in salt between Nepal and Tibet. Nepal lacks salt of its own.

A porter, weighed down by the paraphernalia of a high-altitude mountaineering expedition to tackle Putha Hiunchuli at the western end of Dhaulagiri Himal, emerges from deep shadow into the blessed sunlight while crossing a bridge over the Barbung Khola.

Opposite: A homestead near Tibrikot on the Thuli Bheri River. The effigy with arms outstretched guards the entrance while the very substantial ladder, made from a single forest tree, allows access to the roof and will surely last forever and serve the grandchildren of the current inhabitants. The heavy timbers of the upstairs window frames are ornately carved.

Top: Looking across the Thuli Bheri Khola from a vantage point high above Juphal Dainibara, northwest of Dhaulagiri Himal. Track detail, the stream patterns and retaining walls of the terraces are picked out by the sun, and fields of rye and buckwheat add colour to this pre-winter landscape. *Above (Left)*:Two prayer flags, threadbare due to age and the onslaught of the storm winds of winter, pull proudly and cast their shadows on the wall of the building, part of the lamasery that stands on the eastern shore of Phoksumdo Tal, N.W. Nepal. *(Right)*:A carved rooftop effigy stands guard and serves to ward off evil and to protect the homestead throughout the seasons and throughout the night until the power of the Sun-god comes again at dawn.

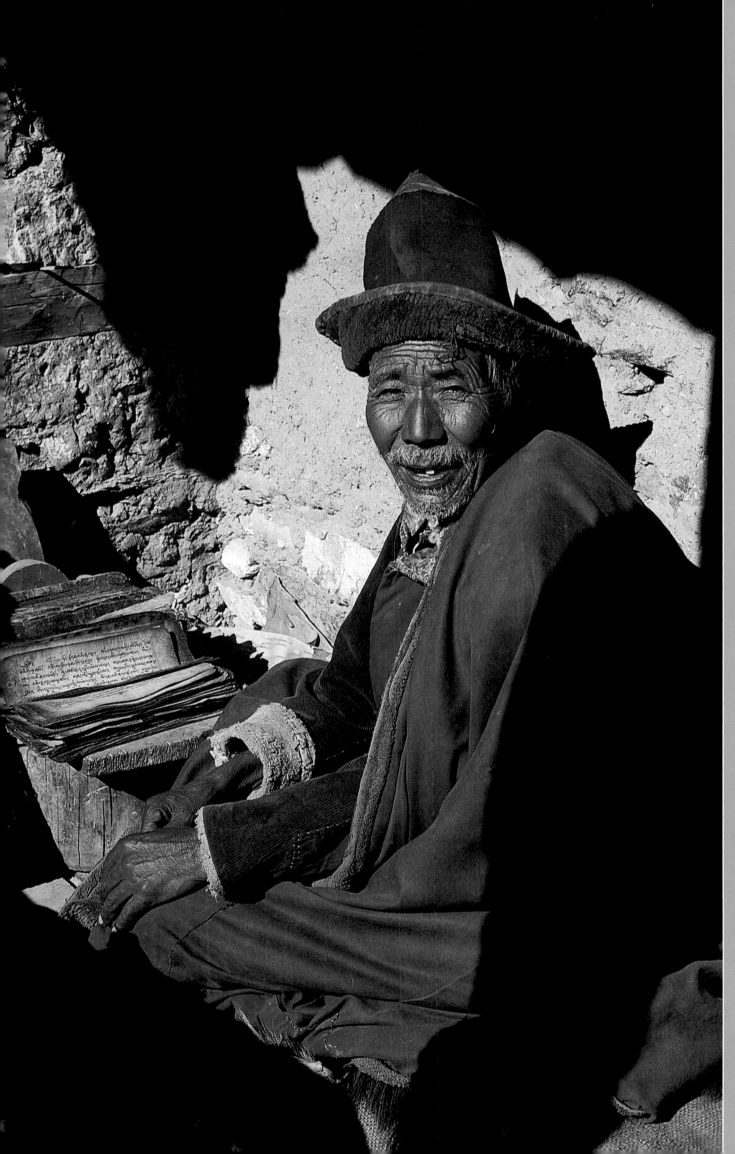

The lama of Ringmigaon seated with his box of well-thumbed and weather-beaten prayer books on the sunlit porch of his tiny, ramshackle lamasery near Phoksumdo Tal.

Left: The author's porters negotiating a staircase built from slabs of mountain rock. They are on the traverse between Dhaulagiri VII and Phoksumdo Lake. *Left (Below)*: It is Dasain when all Hindus celebrate the victory of good over evil. In the picture, the temple at Tibrikot, situated on its rock pinnacle above the Thuli Bheri River, is decked out in all its finery and beneath huge red and white banners of Hinduism.

In the quiet of a Himalayan dawn a flock of mountain sheep grazes the tough grasses close to the lamasery that serves the far-flung homesteads of the people of Tarapgaun on the Tarap River, in high N.W. Nepal.

The sun strengthens to light up the palings of this wooden bridge as well as the coniferous trees and autumnal sedge on the shoreline of Rara Lake, north of Jumla, N.W. Nepal. *Below*: The last of the night mists rise from the banks of the Sinja Khola, allowing the sun to penetrate and light up the autumn colours in the trees and also the green sward of the river banks.

Opposite: The great mass and sun-flushed summit of Kanjelaruwa tower above the ruffled blue-grey waters of Phoksumdo Tal. White Buddhist prayer flags deck the landscape near the Ringmo Lamasery set just above the shore of the lake.

Cho-Oyu: A Mountain in Tibet

The view looking west from Advanced Base Camp on Cho-Oyu. The pass of Yalung-La lies beyond the deep shadow and runs down left and so south to the Solu-Khumbu area of Nepal. Stout-hearted Tibetans move on foot through the frozen snows of the pass to trade with Namche Bazar in Nepal. The Base Camp tents are set up on the morainic debris that covers the moving, living ice of the northern Cho-Oyu Glacier.

The Sun-god lights up this prayer flag set on an altar at the Cho-Oyu Advanced Base Camp. In the background, late autumn winds lift a large banner cloud from the summit of the mountain. *Opposite (Above)*: Cho-Oyu in a savage mood with the jet stream tearing at its summit. *(Below)*: The mountain in a quieter mood and with thick condensation mists clogging its lower flanks. A telescope points at the mountain and allows those at Advanced Base to follow their colleagues' progress throughout most of the action high up on Cho-Oyu.

Looking north and so further into Tibet from the Cho-Oyu Advanced Base Camp. Climbers' tents dot the surface of this lateral moraine and a radio antenna provides a link with the outside world.

Opposite: The day is well advanced at Base Camp and the sun lights up tents and prayer flags as well as the jumbled ice blocks and the mounds of snow-covered morainic debris that lie beyond and below the tents. The flanking mountain summit is capped with spectacular arêtes as well as cornices, hanging ice fields and snow ridges delicately fluted by prevailing winds.

Phinja Sherpa, his face burnt black by the summit sun on Cho-Oyu. His face is whiter where his oxygen mask and high-altitude goggles protected his skin from the sun's glare and gives him a racoon-type appearance. The strain of the ascent (and then descent with a snow-blind lady climber) are evident in his face.

Opposite: Sherpa *Sirdar* Ang Passang at Cho-Oyu Advanced Base Camp after reaching the summit with his team. The sun flares off the sun glasses of this extremely capable, confident and experienced mountaineer. Cho-Oyu is the sixth highest mountain in the world.

Everest (Chomolungma)

Sunrise at Everest Base Camp as seen from the foot of the Khumbu Icefall. The sun sparkles off the ice of this close-up of a minor pressure-ridge in the Icefall to produce a spectacular display. The lowering sky is full of the threat of snow.

The early dawn light begins to light up the tents at Base Camp and clouds of fragrant smoke from juniper fires lit by Sherpas as offerings to the spirits of the mountain, fill the air. In the foreground, the ice of the Khumbu Glacier, awash with morainic debris and boulders, ablates to form ice-pillars where rocks and stones have protected the ice from the sun's rays. *Below (Left)*: Dawa Gyalzen, cook extraordinaire, who lived at Camp 2 at 21,300 ft for almost three months and produced meals there despite the conditions and even when the jet stream and a mother of all storms almost destroyed Camp 2 as he sat in it. *(Centre)*: Manbahadur Tamang at Base Camp prior to an attempt on the summit. Pumo Ri, this spectacular outlier of Everest, is in the distance. Manbahadur, both as a high-altitude climbing Sherpa and in the role of *Sirdar* has now summited Chomolungma several times. *(Right)*: Tough and enduring, Nawang Sherpa at Base Camp after the successful summit bid.

The early light picks out and enhances the angles, the vertical rock walls and the spectacular upper slopes of Lingtren. Spawned by the power of the Sun-god, spectacular avalanches plunge down its massive slopes. Lingtren shuts in Everest Base Camp from the west.

Top: Coloured prayer flags hang limp at dawn and veil the tents of an expedition at Base Camp set at 17,600ft on the moving ice of the Khumbu Glacier. *Above (Left)*: The sun rises from behind the great West Ridge of Everest and flares behind the prayer flags and national flags of this altar. Smoke from green juniper twigs rises from the altar built by the expedition's Sherpas and blessed by lamas prior to the expedition setting foot on Chomolungma. *(Right)*: Tshering Sherpa, with multiple summit successes to his credit as a lead Sherpa with expeditions on Mount Everest.
Opposite: Looking out beyond the chilli sauce bottle and the expedition's mess tent, a Sherpa and a Sherpani (lady) trader can be seen debating the cost of two sackfuls of fresh juniper twigs.

Looking up the line of the Marsyandi River towards Manang Village. The stark cliffs mark a point of rejuvenation and so of enhanced down-cutting and erosion by the river. Further up, the valley opens up and the mountains stand back sufficiently to allow aircraft to land at the airstrip at Ongdi – but only in the early mornings before the very strong adiabatic winds of late morning sweep up the valley to make flying a hazardous venture.

Above: The sun is momentarily trapped behind the wooden roof tiles of two wayside *chortens* (shrines) near Braga in the Manang Valley. *Right*: A juniper fire is lit to provide incense and spiritual inspiration as believers perambulate their sacred prayer walls in the rays of an early sun. *Far right*: Tall Buddhist prayer flags dot the entire religious landscape of the Manang Valley and are to be found decking out even the most inaccessible of rock outcrops and rugged crags. The flags pull incessantly in the wind and so scatter prayers everywhere. The flags also mark the routes uphill and act to spur on any believers who might tire on the steeper gradients.

The Manang Valley

Sunlight penetrates the narrow lanes of the old part of Manang Village and picks out details of a doorway built many, many decades ago. Such character does not exist in the doorways of newer lodges that now dominate the lower end of the village. *Right*: Carved out of the living rock, the trail to Manang is perched high above the ice-cold, silt-laden waters of the upper reaches of the Marsyandi River.

Opposite: The sculpted face of Annapurna III seen from the Manang Valley. Arêtes and cornices abut everywhere and the path of the northern glacier down through the forested lateral moraines can clearly be seen. With access to the summit so difficult from this northern side, attempts on the mountain are normally done from the southern side.

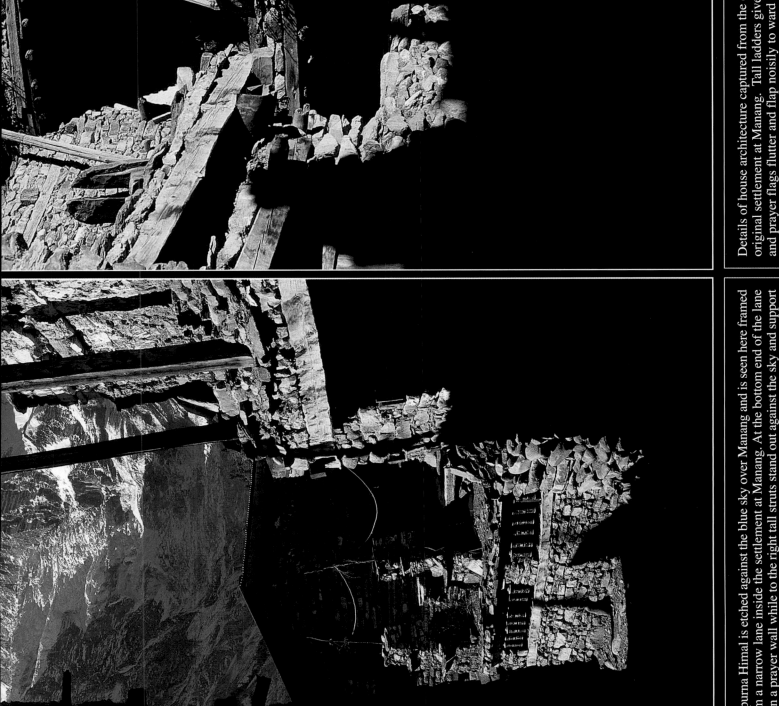

Details of house architecture captured from the centre of the maze of buildings that make up the original settlement at Manang. Tall ladders give access to upper floors, granaries and to the roofs and prayer flags flutter and flap noisily to ward off evil and (equally) to remind the devout about their duties and obligations.

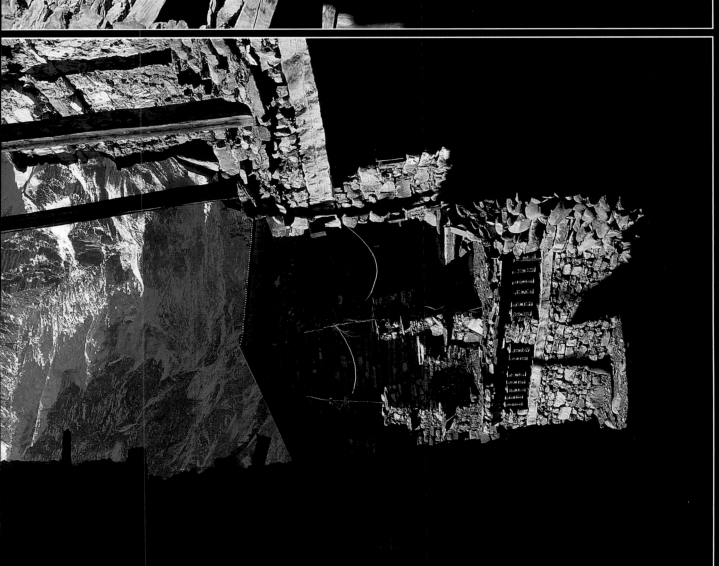

The summit of Gangapurna Himal is etched against the blue sky over Manang and is seen here framed through buildings from a narrow lane inside the settlement at Manang. At the bottom end of the lane are prayer wheels set in a prayer wall while to the right tall struts stand out against the sky and support a roof over a *chorten* beneath which people can walk. The roof protects the *chorten* from the ravages of wind, snow and ice.

The sun floods onto the cleared rice terraces at Takum-Sibang on the Myangdi Khola, en route Dhorpatan. Rice stubble still lies in some fields and in others piles of manure have been got ready to be spread prior to ploughing for the planting of the winter crops of wheat and barley.

Below: It is the time of *Tihar* – the Festival of Light – and houses, bridges, water-points, flights of rice terraces and areas prone to landslip and disaster, are each festooned with garlands made out of leaves and flowers to protect them from evil spirits and to appease the deities. In the picture the detail of one such garland can be seen. The sun lights up the leaves and flowers of the garland against the black of the valley, still in deep shadow, down below.

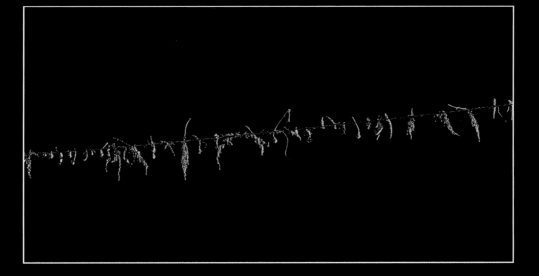

During the major 10-day rice-harvest festival of *Dasain*, when evil is defeated and the victory of good and purity celebrated, villages build tall swings out of wood or bamboo as part of the general merrymaking. In the picture, the sun lights up a swing in the village of Lumsum at the foot of the Jalja-La Pass. By way of blessing, the top of the swing is decorated with garlands of flowers and white and red strips of cloth.

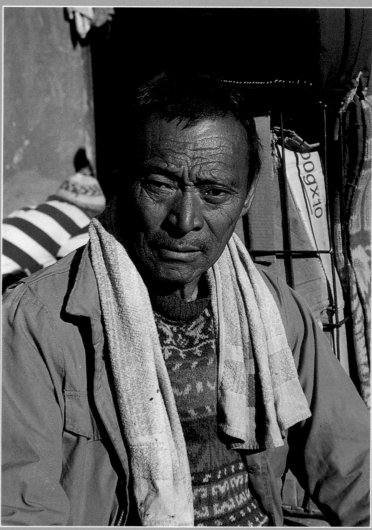

Morning light floods the valley of the Myangdi Khola and traces out sets of rich, fertile terraces just north of Durbang. *Bottom*: The Sungod strikes the gable of this isolated homestead near Lumsum and brings warmth, light, happiness and hope to all who reside within.

Opposite (*Top Left*): The Magar shepherd of Dhorpatan: to ward off the thick frosts that cover the ground of the Dhorpatan Plain throughout much of the year, the shepherd has his hill blanket pulled tightly around him. The blanket has a hood and the wool of the blanket, matted and kneaded together by the weavers who work the wool with their feet, is exceptionally warm and the natural oil left in the wool makes the blanket waterproof. Many a shepherd has woken at dawn with his hair white from frost but his body warm and dry within the folds of his blanket. *Top Right*: A small Magar boy in a much lighter type of hill blanket. He is still wearing the earrings of his youth, one belief being that the piercing of his ears to carry earrings causes blemishes to his person and that no wizard, witch, evil spirit or hobgoblin would ever steal such a blemished child away. *Bottom Left*: The blacksmith's son by the waters of the Buji Khola that drains south from the Dhorpatan Plain. Elf-like, he will fish the waters of the river for his breakfast. *Bottom Right*: A professional porter rests awhile by a homestead before the next haul up towards the pass. In the pass, he will rest again before the long descent to the markets on the plains.

THE GURKHAS

Into The Regiments

The boys depicted in the next few pages were born to be soldiers. Soldiering is in their blood and their upbringings in the harsh, demanding environment into which they were born have toughened their bodies and minds. They have all, each one of them, achieved that first great victory in life for a youngster in the hills of Nepal: they have survived to see the age of puberty. For a Gurkha boy, the second great victory in life is to be recruited. The boys have heard the battle stories of their elders as told round the fire by night or by day with the sun heating up the walls of the village courtyards as the elders recount exotic tales of battles lost and battles won. And so now, with razor-sharp eyesights and their minds on fire with anticipation, the boys scan the trails leading to their homes, watching for the *gallawala* (recruiter) to arrive. For it is he who holds the key that will enable them to have their dreams come true: to be able, like their grandfathers, fathers, uncles, elder brothers and other members of their closely-knit kin groups, to get into uniform and serve in a British regiment out across the black water far, far from home.

Above (*Left*): A Tamang shepherd boy huddles into his hill blanket against the cold of dawn. (*Right*): A bundle of mischief waiting to be recruited. *Opposite*: This young Gurung boy has been garlanded by his sister during the festival of *Bhai Tika* when sisters worship brothers. Gilung

While they await the arrival of maturity and the minimum age to be taken off as 'would-be' soldiers, the boys are put to many tasks. *Khukuri* or *khurpa* (sickle) in hand, they comb the forests and hillsides for loads of firewood and fodder. They also make long carries with baskets of food and flour to upland grazing grounds or go with their fathers to collect heavy loads of salt and paraffin on the annual economic pilgrimage to lowland bazaars. They also tend their father's flocks, plough the land, repair the padi walls and, in quieter moments, look after baby brothers and sisters. The boys grow up, then, as confident, independent spirits, knowing that they are the equals of their environment. They are tough and resilient, are inured to heat and cold, hunger and thirst, and have razor-sharp senses. They are all hunters and can move across ground like wraiths...excellent attributes for any 'would-be' soldiers to have.

Top (Left): The marvellous smile of that 'porter extraordinaire' – Dawa Tamang. *Top (Right)*: A small red-coated leprechaun waiting for luck to turn up. Bhurtibang, W. Nepal. *Bottom (Left)*: Still wet from the waters of the Modi Khola, a young Magar dries off in the sun beside his father's large *doko* (carrying basket). *Bottom (Right)*: A Gurung boy at the village water-point. He will carry the heavy vessel up to his homestead and then tend his goats before the long uphill journey to the village school set high in the pass above his village. *Opposite*: A Magar boy of Lukum Gaun, W. Nepal. He is wearing the traditional homespun garment that, crossed and knotted over the shoulders, hangs down in a large pocket-fold to the rear. The garment, worn by

Opposite Top (Left): His uncle a Gurkha Major in a famous regiment, this small Limbu boy cannot
wait to grow up and follow in his uncle's footsteps. *Top (Right)* :A diminutive Ghale boy is decked
out in red and tartan garments sent home to him by an elder brother serving overseas. *Bottom (Left)*:
Not at all sure about the safety of photography, this little Thapa boy still wears his earrings to ward
off evil…Might the earrings just also work against photography…? *Bottom (Right)*: A tough, young
Tamang, sickle in hand, returns homeward having spent the morning cutting fodder for his animals.

The Selection Process

One of the physical tests given to potential recruits in Nepal as part of the recruitment process, is the 'Doko Carry' when recruits are asked to carry heavily-laden carrying-baskets (dokos) against the clock up a very steep hillside on a route made up of rough mountain track interspersed with flights of steep, stone steps. The dokos are full of large stones and each doko weighs 35kgs. The baskets are very exactly monitored and are weighed both at the start and finish to ensure that none of the load has been jettisoned anywhere en route.

Above: On the start-line, all eyes on the starter. Opposite Top (Left): At the summit: a hand goes out to clutch a disc from an official as the finishing-point is crossed. Top (Right): Total exhaustion as the punishing headstrap is slipped off. Bottom (Left): The check-weigh to ensure that the correct weight has been carried: a potential recruit wills the scales to register correctly and show "35kgs." Bottom (Right): Happiness flows from the face of this youngster for he now knows he has passed selection and so is now a lahure or 'enlisted man' and is thus well on his way towards gaining a place in his father's regiment.

In Training

As young recruits, Gurkhas train with an eagerness and enthusiasm that leave those who watch them, breathless. They are patiently taken in hand by their instructors who, with dedication and determination, eradicate faults in their young protégés and hone them towards perfection. A Gurkha knows instinctively that to remain in uniform and to come through battle unscathed, he has at all times to be a zealous professional.

Above: Gurkhas are all natural hunters and, wraith-like, are adept at moving towards their prey unseen and unheard. Recruit Gopal Rai during training in fieldcraft. *Opposite Top (Left)*: Amidst clouds of tear gas, recruits undergo training for civil security duties. *Top (Right)*: Recruit Chandrabahadur Thapa, drenched in sweat at the end of a long approach march in full battle gear and against the clock. *Bottom (Left)*: Recruit Indrabahadur Thapa in training gloves: boxing and full-contact karate toughen the bodies and enhance the physical and mental resilience of recruits as they undergo nine months of basic training. *Bottom (Right)*: Perfecting his rifle drill, Chandrabahadur Magar seeks to perform his drill with a style and vigour that would meet the approval of his father and uncles who served before him.

The Finished Article

In the morning sun in the drillshed at Mount Vernon Camp, Singapore, Police Constable Rambahadur Gurung of the Gurkha Contingent parades for duty. *Opposite*: Sergeant Buddhibahadur Gurung, his hat, felt, Gurkha at a jaunty angle, parades as Guard Commander with the Gurkha Contingent of the Singapore Police Force.

Going Home

Once every three years a Gurkha is entitled to home leave when, for six months, he is free to be a Hillman again. Gurkhas husband their savings well as they each know that one day they must return to their Homeland and settle there. And so life is a race against time and is about accumulating money and using it wisely before the nightmare of redundancy or retirement. His first or second home leave, a Gurkha will devote to seeking a bride. Thereafter, home leaves are about land purchases and house construction.

Right: Corporal Yambahadur Ghale going home in snow in the high pass between the Buri Gandaki River and his home village of Barpak, W. Nepal. *Below*: The young Pahalbahadur Gharti Magar of Rukum, home on his first leave and with his kit and equipment neatly slung, bargains here for *mulas* (radishes) with an elderly wayside vegetable seller. *Opposite (Top)*: With the morning sun in their faces, a group of porters and friends carry the belongings of a soldier returning on home leave. They are in a pass above the Arun River, E. Nepal and are about to make the long descent to Num. *(Bottom)*: With their backs to the camera, a soldier on home leave and his two companions talk to four hunter-gatherers they have happened across near the headwaters of the Chilime Khola near Ganesh Himal. The hunter-gatherers are tough, enduring men and here carry baskets full of medicinal roots they have dug up and will now sell down in the plains of India.

Those Who Were Left Behind

Brought up in extended families and closely-knit clan and village groupings, Gurkhas serving away from home never forget those whom they left behind ...

Top: Waiting to grow up, the diminutive Bhanuman Ale of Kalipa Gaun, E. Nepal. *Above*: A young Ale youth in full Nepali national dress at his home in Kalipa Gaun above the Tamar Khola, E. Nepal. He was able to further his education by means of monies sent home by his elder brother who was taken off by a *gallawala* to serve in a Gurkha Regiment of the British Army. *Opposite Top (Left)*: A Ghale boy from the highly nucleated village of Barpak, Darondi Khola, W. Nepal. *Top (Right)*: Seen sitting here on the prow of a ferryboat made from a single forest tree, this small Magar boy helps man the ferry-point on the great Krishna Gandaki River near where the river bends south to break through the Siwalic Hills towards the Terai and so the plains of India. *Bottom (Left)*: A Gurung youth with his *bakkhu* (his thick hill blanket-cum-greatcoat) rests beside the trail near Keronja on the high route between Gorkha and Trisuli Bazaar. *Bottom (Right)*: It is early spring and this Gurung boy is out with his father's plough ready to prepare the padi fields for the planting of the annual maize crop.

Top (Left): Now a widow, this mother, a Raini, followed the drum and accompanied her soldier husband to several parts of S.E.Asia. *Top (Right)*: A young Puneni sister on the verandah of her uncle's lodge at Ghorepani, W. Nepal. *Above*: A small, elf-like brother out with his father's flocks on the Milke Danda in E. Nepal. With his Limbu *khukuri* firmly strapped to his waist, he is an independent spirit, is self-reliant and knows that when the recruiter comes, there will be none better than he himself to go forward as a potential recruit. *Opposite*: The Gurungseni matriarch of the small Gurung village that nestles just below the short gravel airstrip that serves Taplejung in E. Nepal.

Above: A younger brother churning butter at the family homestead. He too, wants to be a soldier one day. Deorali, W. Nepal.
Above (Right): A mother and a small 'would-be' soldier on the sun-lit porch of the Gurung village of Anpu, on the Madi Khola, W. Nepal. *Right*: Well muffled up against the cold of winter winds blowing down from Baudha Himal, this Gurung mother wears the tartan shawl sent home to her by her eldest son and awaits his every return… Barpak, Darondi Khola, W. Nepal.
Opposite: A soldier's mother-in-law greets the early morning sun outside her home. A widow, she lives alone.

Top Row (Left): A Bura Magar boy from Tamangaon, here with his father's *khukuri*. *(Centre)*: An elder brother and professional porter, here portering with an expedition to Makalu. *(Right)*: On pension after a full career in a Gurkha Regiment, this Gurkha Officer now tends his land and animals at Bhumdi Gaun, Syangja, W. Nepal. *Bottom Row (Left)*: The brother who trades in salt. *(Centre)*: The patriarch of Bhurtibang dressed in his hill wrap. *(Right)*: The drummer-boy of Kolma. *Opposite*: The youngest sister who was left behind. Sickle in hand and with her carrying basket set behind her, she rests awhile on the large bare rock that lies just below her house before setting off for the forest to cut grass for her animals.

His axe on his shoulder and life's scars etched into his face, this former soldier turns towards the forest once more. Without firewood, his home would be bereft of light, warmth and hot food.

Honorary Captain (GCO) Bhaktabahadur Gurung IDSM in the pass above his home in Kuduli, Syangja, W. Nepal. He won the Indian Distinguished Service Medal while serving with the 5th Royal Gurkha Rifles, an illustrious Gurkha Regiment of which he was Subedar Major, the top rank attainable by a Gurkha Officer in any Gurkha Regiment. To the north, the cold winds of winter raise banner clouds from the summits of Annapurna and Varaha Shikhar. These same cold winds cause tears in the old soldier's eyes.

  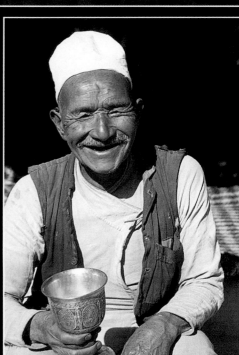

Left: The childless widow of Anpu Gaun drinks a glass of tea provided by a neighbour. *Middle*: The morning sun lights up the wrinkled countenance of an old warrior as he seeks warmth from the sun-heated walls of his home. *Right*: His favourite drinking vessel to hand, an old Limbu celebrates his birthday at Wasun, near the Tamar Khola, E. Nepal. He is 84 and so has now seen 'a thousand moons.'

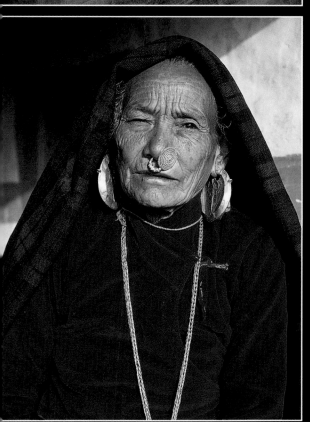

Top (Left): From the dark interior of his homestead in Dadragaun, an old warrior gazes pensively out across his fields towards the snows of Annapurna and Hiunchuli. A decorated Gurkha Officer, he served in battle in World War II with his Regiment, the 5th Royal Gurkha Rifles. Each dawn, heavy brass binoculars round his neck, he patrols his mountain territory as if still on active service. *Top (Right)*: A mother with her white shawl in graceful folds about her shoulders. She is from the Gurung Village of Bhumdi, set on the hills high above Lake Fewa near Pokhara. *Bottom (Left)*: The former venerable matriarch of Khamlalung, a Limbu village set in a saddle of the Milke Danda, Limbuan. She was the mother of (the late) Honorary Captain (GCO) Bhagisor Limbu MVO, MBE, MC — that stalwart of the Tenth Gurkha Rifles. *Bottom (Right)*: Using his army wool shirt and heavy military greatcoat to keep out the cold, this pensioner from Bejang on the Andhi Khola is about to leave home to collect his service pension from a pension–paying post. *Opposite*: An old Tamangseni whose village looks out onto the snows of Ganesh and Paldor Himals. Now too old to climb up to her family homestead, she lives alone in a small hut down near the river and the village water mill.

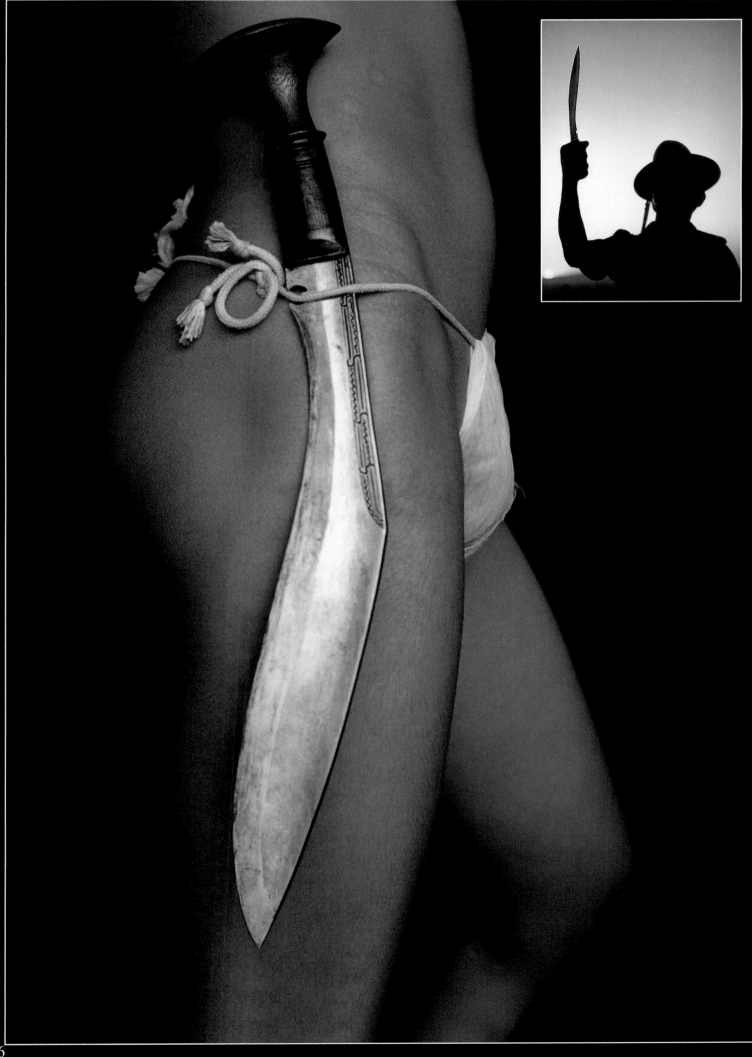

It is late evening in 1961 in a homestead in a village in East Nepal. A Limbu youth has been out ploughing his father's land by day and has now returned home. He has washed at the water point and changed into a clean loincloth before entering to settle by the warmth of the fire-pit to take his evening meal of rice. He has casually slipped his *khukuri* into his waist cord and suspended it there by means of the small knotch at the top of the inner cutting edge of the blade of the *khukuri*, just below the handle. This knotch is, of course, a fertility symbol.

The *khukuri* has been taken by generations of Gurkhas out from their Homeland across the *kalo pani* (the black water) to battlefields all over the world and is an emblem of the hill Gurkha as a fighting man. So also is the 'hat, felt, Gurkha,' worn by all Gurkhas with the panache of men proud of being what they are.

And, of course, there is that certain Gurkha smile…

Top: Sergeant Jahajit Rai 1/10th Gurkha Rifles returned after a long cross-border patrol out from his base at Sungei Tenggang in Sarawak. *Right*: The young rifleman, Bhabiraj Pun, of the Gurkha Independent Parachute Company. His hat, felt Gurkha proudly carries the badge of the Parachute Brigade set against the colours of the Brigade of Gurkhas. *Below*: An old soldier, *khukuri* at the ready and still wearing his trademark rifle-green regimental blazer, sits on his porch and dreams his dreams. His pensive face lights up whenever he meets other old soldiers and, memory jolted, images of himself as a young man on active service begin to flood back…

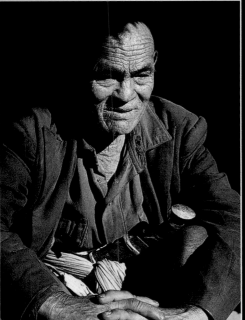

Against the blue of the Tibetan sky, Cho-Oyu flies it's banner cloud. The summit of the mountain is seen here above the green fabric of a mountaineer's tent. A thin layer of ice has formed on the fabric of the tent overnight and this ice now steams in the cold air as the power of the sun re-asserts itself.

And so let us leave the Gurkhas round their camp fires where, with their impish sense of fun and much laughter, they tell the stories that Gurkhas tell. As they talk, their marvellous white teeth gleam in the firelight. When the fires die they will seek out their rough sleeping places and then, with tomorrow's orders clear - crystal clear - in their uncomplicated minds, they will sleep the sleep of children until the next dawn, the next reveille and the next call to duty.

The reds and golds of early autumn light up this swathe of coniferous trees set deep in a side-tributary of the Buri Gandaki River, east of Manaslu.